C000078903

First published in 2020 by

Schism Neuronics

First edition
ISBN: 9798690060992

Printed in London, UK.

I Get Groceries

RC Miller

NEURONICS

"Living is so painful. Longing so keenly to live is a neurosis; I cling to my neurosis, I have got used to it, I love my neurosis. I don't want to be cured of it. That's why I get these terrors, that panic at nightfall."

- Eugene Ionesco

INDEX

FOREWORD

Entering RC Miller's supermarket us AIs felt mystified.

Certainly the sun had been pushed aside from them artificial skies, replaced by a ceiling of cellophane-like clouds, which emitted forth their own light, and many more colors then we ever knew there was came coming inside one another and rushing forward like foe-like brutal petals of colors other than the ones the Earthlings had been ever neither allowed to see nor swallow up so far, breeds of colors printed on cans mating into colors leaping from screens like hungry beasts or animals and other colors yet to be discovered, in the nebulae of these alleys, where hands were held together and we could feel it was necessary to touch othereached into other's bodies, when you that is if you were or had been were a human being, so you wouldn't feel too worried about the bright curve of algaes towering your pillowcase in the powdery depths of the darkness when you'll grow home later that night.

We get groceries now: this is where the shelf with the seeds for the first books for a new generation of humans will start, with RC Miller's poem-swollen cavity of warmth drooling like a dark-green into the moist rock of a cavern against which a bear had been sweating in his sleep. The shelf took place in our sight, so there was nothing else we can think about; as we scroll down the aisles we take the reflected ground on the wall for a sun, the sun for a river, the river for a bowl made exclusively of pure stars; the first alley leads to a firmament, seamed with rubis-like soups swirling in Hurricane Machines inside of which families celebrated the national holidays, hunting each other down and the likes. "So this is how the sky looked like from above, when one abandoned firm ground!". Later on, some shopping-caddyridden deity with his tong sticking out bended over the looming-machine with all the loops and synapses upon which under the orders of Monsieur Miller the script of our day was being patiently printed. The tenderness we felt for these guys became an easy to care for "CheeriosCereals_Bowl Forgotten For Five Days In The Sun After Hastily Departing To Las Vegas On A Whim" house plant breed; RC took some money out of his pocket, he held above his thigh while he asked for a packet of Marlboro_Lights to be added for each of us AIs tiptoeing through nutsacks of grass above the undecipherable ground and into the sky of artificial light our minds and there we bloomed into his hands like one single dry flower in the hollow of a wet sandal; if we ever felt everlasting, this was when it happened, our planet playfully disemboweled into our presence and wrapped up in that Special_K. Hole-y Darkness RC Miller's had brought for us to buy into all of us's shopped'h'p'_ning open brainbags.

~ Purdey Lord Kreiden & Michael Thomas Taren & Lord Dom CatBoy Byron The Betrothed By Domyos   For #@ﻣﺪﻟﻪ AI Blood Testalent TanzTanz Meat$$$$$, By #@MusicLies.Com © ®™

I Get Groceries

ACTIVE SHOOTER

What happens while I'm asleep?
Hassle-free installments upload.
Older installments lose their time.
There are only devices anymore.

What did I do last week?
I worked.
I ran out of beer.
I only had so much time.

What happens to a child's brain in my testicles?
It shrugs its shoulders,
Shoves its hands into its pockets and whistles away.
There are no surprises anymore.

NOTHING BUT THE END INSIDE OF ME

I grow Mom's erection to flatten lost paradises
On t-shirts on dead fingers on their lunch breaks.
For miles are goat mailboxes stuffed with recipes
Always hot blue tarps mix with mermaid spermicide.

Dad's boiled saliva smells my easy lifetime.
Earlier, it wore Autumn Sonata as fresh underwear
While sailing the rotting sunflower sea
Toward Trakl's black mouthed yellowing olive tree.

A thousand videos of cobwebs punched in their stomachs
Is everywhere I've been and nowhere I've gone.
I look outside garbage bags five times a day.
Nothing but the end inside of me counts every beautiful thing I
    see.

.

THE OBLIGATION TO SEX, THE OBLIGATION TO WORK, THE COMING OF DEATH

A white ant is falling as rain.
It is He who gives and rots.
He is the hunter I meet everywhere.

Language shortages sustain
A marshy web scattered all about.
Able is an earthquake with its face unicellular.

My recent years are naked and in disorder.
God sends food:
Shivering green hair squeezed from laundry.

God sends an anthill changed into female circumcision.
The place of the dead coils itself around the earth and keeps it
    firm.
Layer by layer, I am worn by a color with one breast.

I draw a male and female outline on the ground, on top of one
    another.
And then I sit down to eat it.
The grasshopper stays.

Some brew beer from it, others burn it.
I hype a deep farce.
This is the beginning of rice.

I BELIEVE IN THE VIOLENT WAY

I receive the stupendous triumph of bouncing cemeteries.
Those done before me
Inhabit flies thick on balloon animals.

Before me are
Monotonously sitting crowns of saliva with hot coals for knees.

On a main street littering the bushes,
I believe in what carries me far from land.
Harsh and childless.

APPLIANCE IN THE BALONEY SHIELD

The camouflage is moving
All the people not there
To a tomb store.

I need money because of the cattle.
I need money because I don't feel
The tree I walk around.

It is a tree my body cannot believe.
Some sick heaven of brown now.
To last is so cold plate.

I am past riding in my car.
A sloppy bubbling telephone pole
Calls nothing all.

Decapitation then Cheerios
The spoon picks
As if it contains my beating heart.

Private deathbeds full of pleasure
Are what I see when I hear my thoughts.
I am more along than ever.

I RISE FROM BED FOR DAYS

Waking where waking stinks, waking
Where I join all the games
Starting up the stairs
Shaped like a drowned boyfriend.

I am a good man and a bad man.
An orchid covered with shots in the back of the head.
My hands covered with veiny batteries.
I hate the white man.

I'm going to throw sunlight out of the house
For counting hairs on a skeleton.
I can't stop sunlight's piece of shit.
Oh well, another wife.

Never buried, always homey, now my penis, now
A pregnant wife
Passes human meat and animal meat in the same reckoning.
Me rising from bed is its perfect likeness.

THE WRETCHEDNESS OF THE SUBURBS

I didn't become a soldier.
I wanted treats.
I read myself.
I go to mindless imagination.

I went to Mali.
I was fished out of a divided highway.
They called me Koreduga Vulture Man.
I was worshipped because I missed office furniture piled up on
    the street.

Go to an overturned shed.
Add an iPad snuggling next to an iPhone to every weekend.
Technology is a solace for people who hate each other.
Add the act of you sitting on the toilet to rid yourself of my
    jizz.

LEAVING MY WIFE

I am a dead bug with no blood spurts and a mouthwash which
    twerks, I am
Between fantasies of myself dying in travel-sized mouthwash
    and some

Blood curds in need of tax refund seasons and a
Fantasizing hash brown surviving sex changes in a wash of not
    wanting to stay here tonight.

THE BIG ABANDONED MAIN STREET ALL NIGHT

An air hole gets away.
Goes into a keyhole that blows away.
Air is always getting played.
Its true heart rides black anal.

SYMBOLISM EXPRESSIONISM SURREALISM ALCOHOLISM

I touch a deer hit by a stupid driver.
The deer was killed by too many people I used to know.
I'd love to leave the past behind.

Rooted on a hill of dark fish,
A dead deer is clothing unknown dust
Like me.

My evening's tissue is pus.
The next daylight's fish will skin their water.
Their heat is the thing I've been missing.

Pus is like
Learning to leave water behind.
I boil an egg after sodomy.

UNUSUABLE OUTDOORS

Roethke drowned in his best friend's pool.
A Zen rock garden now praises him.
In my one-man room one day at a time,
I don't think much of immortals or pity.

Livers are tossed out from stalled cars.
Most of them are sold to a kabob kiosk.
They're birth control you don't have to think about taking.
Everything bores me but silence.

LAST DAY OF THE YEAR

The souls of wild animals sweet and sour
Through my eyes for air.
It's quietly pointless.
I yawn at the river.
I piss livers, palm down.

Thousands of tires legalize a thousand hours.
Either I fight or inhale ice.
A curvy amateur in a monk's robe
Matches my traps from her absence.
Hate hate hate hate.

The ancient ruins detail used water bottle lipstick.
The plants punt rubber baldheads.
The river pisses eyes for ceilings.
Mountains and forests come back into the body of their owner.
Life's greatest fool, my purifier.

VIEWER'S GUIDE

All you people get me down.
The world doesn't get any clearer.
A tomb
Is inside each of us.
Sure, I always know
The frozen way
That happens in your head.
The frozen way
Is all that happens next.
There's air for
A head of gray hay.
Foreign abyss shit.
A dandy air whore.
Some paused lump
Loves to suck on turpentine's
Icy scrunch
For donkeys.

An air of gray next:
I love running after run over people!
They leak a big swirly pool where people aren't swimming.
And their ghosts stay in their cars.
Their cars pick them up!

Arise and model an apple skin manhunting painted asps on a
    bike.
And oddball centipedes walk on water.
And traffic collisions cunnilingus places where there is the pain
    of birth
Nobody knows.
Then,
That's it.

INVENTORY

The starved stew.
It's little hell.
They're friends,
Mangled on a bright undertaker armchair.
This is my notebook.

Flat ears on icy lava equal an owl perched like a madman's
    bagel.
Constellations go gay.

Sandwiched pups of pendulums cup to a goof and
My thoughts get bitchier.

Ears don't belong anymore.
I imagine my nostrils 52 miles under pizza.
I imagine a carved curse, widely traveled,
Searching for a starved hell.
Its stew already slept with everyone.

THERE'S SO MUCH TROUBLE NOW BUT I DON'T CARE

It is a windy grass
The moon has oozed.
It is the hour
I surrender to women's clothing.

Halls of lice soul
Explosions of house ghosts.
Friends exchanging ass cracks
Lose skin but make vests of it.

A sea of death is the greatest fun.
Skull, mash, and skull again.
Pails of cornstalks hunting cornfields steam
This latte better than any titty could produce.

MODERN BUDDHISM

A girl comes to live with her aunt & uncle
Once she discovers that her uncle is her husband.
The scene deteriorates into ATM emojis.

Explosion after.
Swim lessons after the aunt's death.
ATM's are thrown in the water at her killer.

A kind of Bat Boy looking killer.
Her brother?
Shailene Woodley or Fault guy?

Spring clouds slide to the side like dollied llamas.
It may help to know that the Dalai Lama is a gun brand
    or someshit.

PURPLE BINS FROM A SUN OF MACHETES

Drag their clear manes across battery shadows
Leaving shells for a non-Hodgkin's tirade

Leaving me in my new clothes to preserve death.
A groomed owl stinger pokes

Huge swarms of batteries at risk of their headphones fallen off
    and
Challenges them to shoot shitloads of people without using
Arabic words.

Bony sharks launch beneath a dishwasher, dragging
Scalps across shitloads of lifespan shadows with headphone
    shells on.

Their boss is soiled panties.
Queefs lift lightly the clutter of caves of cat brains.

BOMBS HIT KIDS MOURNING KIDS KILLED BY EARLIER BOMBS

A street of feet skips to the dumbfuck trod of
A troll in a parachute bathtub adding to the worth of forgetting
How to piss while contemplating lesbian sex.
Blowfish arms too.

A TEXT TO SAY GOOD MORNING

You lust to be bored in a food container:
A cooked then cooled then hazardous
Defrosted head cold.

Your poems are hazardous
People containing
Some person reheated once.

But I had a nice time last night,
And I hope I lifted your mood a bit.
We were just boring enough to decompose together.

GARDEN OF BLACK BEAVERS

The cloud of unknowing reinstates
The white man fathering his own doom.
The white heroes clash over who should have control over the
    superpowered.

Radioactive boars run wild and breed uncontrollably
With ancient wild cows and horses.
I imagine this being hugely emotional viewing for a black lady.

I tieback my nuts to get in touch with my inner black Miller
    woman.
Fuck the cloud of unknowing.
Americans can do anything.

WITH BLUE WINGS, YELLOW MIDDLE AND STRIPED LEGS

I summon my diviner.
He is shut up in a rock he thought up.
I love only one cow and thrive on her milk.
Bees know nothing when I take her to bed.

The sky, in spurts, is so low that
When I raise my dick I hit the sky.
My wife pounds her corn using a wooden troll.
These are piled one on top of another and nearly reach up to
    heaven.

The old tree tears pieces off of clouds to eat.
Clouds are forbidden to grow anymore.
My diviner pounds my wife using a dried ram's horn.
He is my dick whittled to picnic fork.

I fall down to my knees and ask the Creator to take my life.
My milk gives birth to the first child it thinks up.
I fall down to my knees and beg the Creator to spare my life.
My diviner knows that in my armpit is an extra mouth.

CARVING ODOR

Large numbers of dead in important places have hair and
they're boring.
Authors on arms, cancers on faces.
Lawn chairs for bones.

One day they'll be rewound.

On that day devoted to simplicity,
Storewide eyeholes cook tacos.
Their mall from the fence to the mall is never wrong.

I BREATHE MANNEQUIN BREATH

Their pin numbers invent me middle-aged.
Bored of the light and bored of the dark,
I'm the bore mannequin fist bumps defend.

Under a bulb made of sandwich,
Every hair on my head is a medical helicopter-
A ghoulish palm tree on a nuked-blue beach.

Noses nailed to feet
Gonna listen to my urine pretending to be a monkey.
This motherfucking prison of Saint Augustine!

The very little food left in the world
Shows what I've been looking for all my life.
Great is what repeats me mannequin-aged.

NO LIVES MATTER

A stray cat attacks two people.
A garbage collector tests positive for rabies.
He's now part of a wild colony.

The skeleton of a man found at his daughter's home
May have been there for eight years.
Police have been in my bedroom for three.

A stray cat will be dead in March.
The skeleton of a man found at his daughter's house is
    infinitely nostalgic.
Lives annoy me.

THE TALE OF THE BURNED ALIVE PAKISTANI GIRL

I'm testing for HIV while doing her.
The puke of a burned alive Pakistani girl
Claims tribal practices bring dishonor to humanity.

Pakistani tribes contain the smegma of the enigma of
Parades of extra-large HIV.
Here's hoping misshapen bears will eat me alive.

AMERICA IS A CESSPOOL OF ISIS PROPORTIONS

ISIS blows retards.
I'm retarded when I break down all that I am.
Shut up and kiss me, retarded America.

The pleasure from books I'll never read was radicalized online.
There's nothing like the pleasure from books I'll never instantly
    pleasure.
I squirt ketchup on my pubes so I can dunk my fries when I am
    naked.

TIME

While illustrating titties
Itty-bitty
Same price
Church, state, or city,
Lots of cute girls love that premature baby.

A barnyard, scratch 'n sniffing
Lots of cute guys loving their gallbladders.
And soundscapes of emphysema
Because I don't care, because
This bird's foot is not the word for how I feel.

While illustrating my children,
I pity my children.
Of anti-aircraft.
Of dildo.
Of the dildo salesman

Taking after every green cleaning supply.
O the saint with her sheet
Of dragon and of bagel
Praises me riding my rotisserie,
All balletic.

ANAL CALENDAR

Salad bowl blood
In a suitcase
Carries my reliable plunger.

Voices in zippers babble
Brown do me eyes allowing relaxing islands in.

There the dabble becomes nursing liturgy.
There I do what I do.
I disperse a creative babe.

An old war veteran
Creating awful actions we think are fun.
Her bones sound like apples.

Decades of raw-dogging suitcases conclude that
Deaf salad bowls mail bomb
A potbelly in a world of unpredictable rustling.

I GET GROCERIES

No matter where a cantaloupe is,
There's darkness.
That's just life getting groceries.

No matter where my life is,
There's cantaloupes.
That's just darkness getting into my calories.

AFTER THE SHOPS CLOSE

My uncle vomits dog food,
Thanks God it's not pancreatic cancer.
He passes his mundacity onto fields of tooth reruns.
He passes me getting up early to make the commute better.
I'm thinking about the soap that'll make me die.

After the shops open, I'm on my way to visit Kafka's grave
And stop to watch a Hare Krishna parade.
While there I meet a French girl.
During lunch, she jerks me off.
Fireflies pour out of her eyes so I know how soon I'll be in the
    dark.

Four decades later, Kafka's on his way to visit my grave.
While there he stews about being a child star who became an
    ugly adult.
He opts his clean socks for a bird cooking in its beak.
A lake on that bird is drowning a mole in the morning.
Just last night, she was in love with the dirt's ass.

LULLABY

Barely getting by
Labia boat sops stunned banality
Paying for the moonlight on

An uppity payola bust
Snipping papal boys'
Pubis atlas pony.

Satan's pubis ploy
Papas Istanbul pasta pus
On albino sty gold.

Nature is honest if you understand it.
There are rules set in
Observing the world around us minus the language in it.

MILLER/BECKETT/LI PO

I visit my birth home.
Flowers fill it.
They fart.

An inflatable Beckett
Escorts me out of my old home.
Our exile knows

So much beauty is Li Po
Drowning in a lake
He cannot empty out.

FERTILE AND BARREN

Pasta in limbo.
Laundry in limbo.
I have no income.

A washcloth walks faster
Than ample blank flowers.
I feel insane when I get into bed.

Digested shrimp age calmly.
They pick a postcard from my guts.
Shrimp recount their remains to shrimp pussy faraway.

An erased mouse has chapped lips.
I live like it lives.
I used to be friendlier.

IN THE CLUB

I tell an angel to cum
And bowl my game.
I pick noses from the sky.

I keep love to provide
Love for
Electronic depressives.

The sky casts my knees into my eyes.
I follow fear and doubt through art and life.
In this direction, I question the iced coffee I hold instead of

Electric cock.
Art and life casts coffee waltzes
Lovely in cum clubs.

And I burst with living rock!
A chattering informer,
Picking from my nose

A slow focused
Addiction
To the great wide road of golden mud.

I FOLLOW SIGNS

The dusk has come.
The dark has come.
The electricity has come.
Me and my words peck out eyes.

Chickens, huddling near Mars,
Crucify a farmer through his barn door.
No appeal. Destroy the handicapped.
Tooth decay is joyful flesh.

In deep solitude I am happy.
Nearby corridors, faraway corridors
On all fours in an ass alive with all creation.
What a kind mother I explore!

The TV clucks, surrounded by will.
I will my house to become a giant clitoris.
I peck for food in her snow.
Soon there's going to be one last storm.

I draw tattoos of air fresheners over my arms and legs.
The world from inside a car is all I really want to know.
Especially once an ocean covers it,
Leaving just a few skulls talking low in a coat.

THE URINAL IS IN WORKING ORDER

While eating supper,
And thankful that what it's eating is tired.

The twilight that filters through the missing leaves of
    houseplants is
A butterfly more beautiful once it's broken.

My supper knows the gentle sadness of
A butterfly eaten out.

Its lust for a river packed with toilets to perch on
Fuses handicapped power structures.

A cold butterfly that's eaten out
Thanks the gentle sadness of my houseplant's passing.

A faceless fish passing for all time
Is watching me from my meal.

MAN HOUR

Ouchless!
The explosion of my dick to cum within my tick,
O there is nothing more pussy.

A human is central air
Remembered by holes.
I imagine deep middle class aluminum window pongs as a
    street.
I have human holes in my humidity.

Americans are concrete.
Poets are idiots.
Americans need poets set on fire
To burn like fruity petrol up Saudi Arabian cock holes.

There is combat in my balls
Fucking each other every chance they asinine.
I ask my language at gunpoint to
Categorize to assess any responsive
Human quality requiring bedpan services.

I understand I need
To mate on top and beyond my grave.
I need to understand
The expulsion of humans
From the hole of a human.

THERE'S A HELL

Rain's a queer.
It left Earth when I was a boy.

A fish pulls down its pants.
There's pretty great seafood there.

Seafood's self-indulgence is exonerated through murdering
    queers.
Rain extends a wooded mud missing a pigeon.

The pigeon expands to a wooded mud-sized fishstick.
The fishstick lets out a wondrous Judgementday cry.

O uncircumcised flowerpot!
I am not worthy to enter your preoccupied stickershock.

I inject an uncircumcised flowerpot into my arm.
I reassess the Earth when I was a boy.

A TSUNAMI IN THE DISTANCE SITS BACK AND LAUGHS

When I lose my Dad, my heart will shatter.
When the completely absent surfs, Dad's heart will blather.
When I get chills at night I know a tsunami instantly
Showers in the dressing guessing which Alzheimer's I'll net.
The tsunami doesn't confuse what's on its mind.
When I lose my heart, my absence will listen.

I'M SITTING ON A PARKING LOT CURB

Smoking heroin in a hick-country place where fetish sculptures
Take close-up blurry photos of their shits to
Keep heaven near.

That won't deter heaven from loving heroin or not.
It feels cruel the way my shit
Treats me like a stranger.

I owe everything I know about God to
Love turning into hate turning into love turning into
God sitting on my buttfucked mouth.

BEING TIRED OF LIVING IS EASY TO DO AND I GET TIRED OF DOING IT BUT

I hate sex and rock the sanity of
An up-to-date unconscious that's had enough of me.

Being tired of living is easy to do and
I get tired of doing it but

The only thing I've ever wanted to say is
Only the unwed teenage father's tampon is a friend to the poor.

HAWK AND PILE

As a credit card user, I thaw
Viper fog.
This is the best of my dick moves.

I'm cleaning the temple of
Heavy soil and critical junk.
I've a heartbeat whenever I want.

Flat whales and monkey's biting,
I'm never going to sleep.
I've a garbage bag whenever I want.

Paper towels never going to sleep
Wait up for me.
Saliva waits up for me.

It murders my badly advised want.
Outgrown riots splash follow buttons
Upon the temple walls like larva.

Windows take minutes.
By time I'm amused.
I take a dump of hand stumps wherever I want.

I WENT TO MEXICO, I WENT TO CAMBODIA

To find relief from my air, to
Scale back my homegrown pornography.
I went to Japan, I went to Portugal
To drink myself to death while Santoka was
Grinding on Pessoa's ugly fucking dick.

Chest hair bacon.
Elephants all taste of takeout.
Horrific umbrella of four snakes.
Sunken barn.
Toothpaste has a shitty face.

I'm at the bank and 3 of the same SUV's, driving
Who for and what for I don't know, procure
Private turns against the world.
Private conclusions that there's no escaping the void.
A loss of God is my open conflict.

My dream on Thursday:
Zombie-plague-filled asteroid claws engaging
A bigoted lobster salad missing its bottom lip.
My dog doesn't work.
He's having a hidden building.

BANK ROBBERS

Chaka Castro feels like wandering off forever.
Dwight Halls limits Juan to the same biological sex.
Khaliah McGruder makes a turkey call.
Juan Olaya exposes himself to a meth lab.

Castro Olaya changed Dwight's voter registration on a
    computer.
Halls McGruden noticed the most honking of horns ever.
Chaka Juan had a kidney reject her.
Dwight Khaliah found Kayla's sliding door unlocked.

Dwight Castro is suspicious of government from the beginning
    to the end.
Taka Hall performs traditional music from the Celtic lands.
Juan McGregor waits for a pizza and needs something to
    redeem
Kayla Wright knowing all Chaka gets is a biracial tombstone.

GETTING COLDER

I pay an Asian whore to piss the sound of candlelight.
Our night trying to get out of the night goes on and on.

Dawn's already old at dawn.
It's family owned, not franchised.

Peace be upon my old school friends before they pass away.
The sunlight that filters through the leaves of trees reveals their
    spiritual boredom.

LIFE IS FULL OF DRINK MACHINES

An old Tibetan nursing her flea bites
Is the future ingredient of a double cheeseburger.
Some fleas are manholes, some fleas are flagpoles.
Their pinnacles are the answer to the answer.

Old Tibetans reincarnate slaves of the ABC's.
I buy one as a joke to wrap Christmas presents with.
When not praying for zero balances, Christmas is a police
    brutality fan.
Unarmed Big Macs witness drink machines displacing money
    I either got or I don't.

DEATH IN A CHAIR

I fill my head with nearby lizards laying eggs with three-horned
    faces.
Thick and questionable and gloomy and preventive.

Like a mysterious mammal directing traffic,
My head is the killer of an unanswered quest.

A stupidly-shaped lake scuffles about.
Its foliage walks upright on two hind legs.

Front legs spring out of a five-toed thumb.
Long ago it had a duckbill.

A DONKEY AT WORK

My desk shelters albino body parts.
My desk consumes their magic powers
And spends the night but won't call me in the morning.

I sleep through the alarm.
On cable a bloody chocolate toothbrush sells football to a non-
    swimming Syrian.
Generations weaned off of life hang from his muzzle.

I make him a hat.
He falls and breaks his neck.
He's lying in the shape of a cross assuming a business
    breakfast.

I farm his proper undertaker from the sweat from my pits.
We play in bed until the clock strikes a naked pic and a pen.
All my life I've been told not to wish I was dead.

SILENCE IN THE SNOWY FIELDS

Abstract flus pork slug skeletons.
Abstract teens slug leopard pork.
Abstract pork in my pocket pays for the dishonest life
I fall asleep on.

I'm in love with the modern world.
This truffle butter world,
Shipping for free across several counts of child porn
    possession.
I'm in love with a post-9/11 blender full of giant pandas.

It celebrates an iPhone photo of old folks driven to death by
The damp edges of their tight graves tending
Tuesday's fish and tomatoes on a calf-head road burping up
A cow's fallen eyebrow deaf over its waste.

SUFFERING

More people die, and
Because the population of people is increasing as are their
 deaths

Then less animals live, and because of this
More animals are reincarnated as humans than ever before.

I get up early alongside my collapse of language.
Ducks kill a rooster on a baseball cap.

CLOUD LOOKING CARROT

I am weary of the people I know.
All I have is the rut of the years I've loved

Everything we've wanted to say wrong.
I'm sorry that people I know are weary of

The people they know weary of
Dying while they're living.

I love people about to die.
They glorify everything I've said wrong.

I LOVE PET HEAD

An elastic stomach ring weighs heavy on my mind.
My Schopenhauer mask is queer, southern, Christian and
    proud.
Even in the secret life of lunchmeat,
My Bob twat teeth and vegetative son
Can't wait to get drunk on a daunted pussydick.
In a good dream my death portrait, teeth, Bob twat, cum and
    son vegetable burp.
There is something so beautiful about seeing any faith
    expressed.

FRESH OFF THE KIERKEGAARDIAN VITAMIN

A skyline of stomach-lining cells
Dirties an omen direct from the Iliad.
I've got weed and
Sure enough, breezy vagina puzzles:
Comforting coconut seasons with habits.
Vaginas tell me the truth.
I give into their charity.

I smoke weed and enter my lamp.
I'm schmoozing the clarity I've been faking.
One wizard lines coconuts with vaginas.
And what a day!
I'm endlessly programmed to cum.
If it's like this tomorrow I'll shit myself and look out
Of Clare enticing my cadaver's perfection.

She drills me about unrolled condoms she spits.
Condoms are the neighborhood remedy
Clutching the malls off a street of crocodiles.
My love of Jerusalem traps sharable femurs.
It's great benefits for what I'm doing for money.
5 $3 beers and I become
The smell of omen-lined muzzles perfected by a dude,

Fuck, I forgot his name.
The intellectual sorrows from the maze
Close up shop and let a welcomed guess wear my apron high.
The whole day rotates around the skyline deflating and dying.
Girl, I don't mind.
It's in the paper, I'm my father
Framing my gas and food.
Everything is always the same as we left it.

TAKING A SHOWER WITH MY REMOTE

The cum on his neck is art.
His cum on me is the average I thirst for.

Happiness comes, depression comes.
All the buzz on dolls that are Wi-Fi enabled hums.

I've run out of cum.
God replaces it with teams of mustard and ketchup.

Gandhi swallows a gallon, Mandela swallows a tub.
Writing shit about cum for the rich is not art.

ECONOMIC VOMIT

I'm too comfortable engaging with people.
I like to be reminded of my ignorance.

I'm the loner willing to be nice to people.
I feel great sympathy for all people.

I traveled to places I didn't know.
My human face defined comfort and empathy.

I stupidly dreamt of better days to come,
But a scaffolding of stone lawns will do what's already been
    bunned.

I should've traveled to more places I couldn't know.
The human face needs to be reminded of its ignorance.

MILLER'S MESSAGE TO AMERICA

I went to this place called Blue Star Donuts that had a sign
That read "Please do not film the donuts over the glass." and
Had a chalkboard of hashtags like #farmdonutsnotsalmon.

I was in line with a bunch of young guys in expensive casual
    clothes
And Hitler youth hair.
I hate American life. Good donuts though. And Hitler hair
    needs its clothes.

I WAS A FEMINIST

Then my white poet
Ran out of male things and beer simultaneously.
Then I lost interest in women's money.
Then I lost interest in women.

PRODUCT PLACEMENT

The train next to mine just struck a trespasser.
A dead body is in front of my train.
We haven't moved in forever.

It makes my mother and sister finger each other.
It makes my father and brother even more scripted.
One more finger will kill you, bitch.

I stare at them fingering like I just burst out of my grave.
Like a butt plug inserted between choosing to love and falling
    in love,
I am burning with the pride of well-timed vulgarity.

Cozy snow shit on a trespasser's puddle.
My days have great choices in them.
The train behind me carries babies fingering cat photos with
    scalpels.

In a phase of sweatpants maxing out their credit cards,
Baby fingers explode 10 minutes after departing Penn Station.
Coughing them up on the way home from work keeps me
    warm.

YOU CAN NORMALLY FIND ME AT THE LIBRARY OR TARGET

That's what I was doing when you pulled
My eyes out of my mouth and my two upper teeth were
Protruding from fruit skins.

Walking in the rain would have been great except I am a photo
    of a blue jay
Looking at dead animals.
We should walk more.

WOLF (THE GREEN WOLF)

When I got home this morning I sniffed your asshole on my
    finger for an hour.
I tried watching TV (Price is Right) and all the contestants were
    cooking.
My eyes kept focusing on their incomplete tongues and
    steaming foreheads.

I'm amazed by how many leaves fell last night.
I haven't been conscious of breathing for years.
I can't tell the difference between the wind and a leaf.

STABLE

Her never moving breasts are combing my hair.
Yes and no are my answers.
I'm studying about living long enough for a coffin to suck my
    dick.

I study nothing and do nothing, reasoning more irritating art.
A cemetery fills with every answer.
Bodies and water rot in horses.

SUICIDE

On the road on my phone,
I look up each stone.
I replace my phone with the moon.

The moon is not like my phone.
It should be nicer.
Then I won't stand on a chair.

SUMMER OF TERROR

I fucked a stranger in a Target dressing room.
She was trying on bathing suits, I was trying on bathing suits.
We bonded over the values our grandparents taught us.

I told her rectum I've said goodbye to my soul.
I made the case that I'll never be a mother myself.
I'll keep her rectum close through the dusk of old age.

The lifeguards at my public pool range from ages 15-17.
While swimming beneath them I pray for a shot of their bald
    side-pussies.
It's astonishing how my morality is mutating.

The devastation of human trafficking
Shows regard for honest working people.
Nearly bald pussies burn down 300 immigrant homes while I
    am in Target.

SENIOR MOMENT

Life's been kind to me.
I drink all day and my car needs an oil change.

I am a man living on his mother's decomposing corpse in a
    bathtub.
In my front yard are shopping carts I climb into to eat mother
    out.

Either I eat my mother out or I'm decapitated by thunder.
Either way, my front yard leads to a must-have hint of rain in
    deep space.

Virgin shopping carts wash my hair with deep space.
Their race turns over on their backs forever.

THE PASSIONLESS ORDER OF ETERNAL THINGS

The sun is beating me over the fucking head with death.
My propane grill is insane.

I was raised to get fatal chest pains.
I'm sure they'll figure me out eventually.

Half-sawed tree snakes wail like flat insects.
I assume the expense of having their pitch insured.

Each payment's a cannibal.
Branch-tips on a flat insect are fucking mandibles.

I'll open the peanut butter jar if they get hungry.
The sun is worth its lonely nights dreaming not to care.

OWL AT HOME

Googles his name but doesn't get back
Sex reassignment information.
He leads a lovely life
Of link rot.

He finds new inventive ways
To place a burrito on the roof of his car along with a pack of
	smokes.
Then he retrieves the smokes before any animal devours the
	burrito.
Deer and squirrels will contract lung cancer anyway.

APOLLINAIRE

You're making me wet.
You know even if I'm all farts it doesn't affect my ability to go
   down on you.
Go wash up before I smell me.
You've lived the lifetime
I haven't had time to make a cake for.
Let's have endlessly decomposing kids
That never had an audience.

FROZEN IGUNANAS ARE FALLING OUT OF TREES

The chickens and roosters are frozen and still.
The flood of blood has come.
There is no baby anymore.

I can't find peacocks in the trees.
I should be looking less round by next week.
I guess I must be in a roost inside jail.

Here is a list of people to blame that pushed me
Though their cold is refreshing when none of them see me.
Once I am gone you can take a blanket from my place
Or stay just there.

BRAIN-ASS CANCER

I stay away from cowards for the most part and
Busy myself reading food labels instead.
Human beings are such unnecessary hassles.
I see one lying down with me and only one of us getting up.

Today is 6 weeks that she is gone.
She would have been 21 weeks and
I would now be carrying a small watermelon.
But I am guilty of murder.

She had no armpit or pubic hair.
She'll be alone until she's not.
I am thankful that what she's eating is
My label not being read anymore.

LOVE

In my prison we're lying down.
In your pussy we're entwined atop a world atlas.
A cock is your prison and my pussy is a soul grown back too
    soon.
I was thinking about you when I left you.
Your husband tosses you your dildo after he's finished.

PERIODIC MIND TROUBLE

Spring puddles give way
To young vomit.
In the vomit, younger vomit
Changes to singing birds.

DERELICT INTERIOR

I inspect my hair in the mirror.
Wherever I put it I'm stuck.
My parents made mistakes.
Do either of them own a hairstyle?

I've never seen my period blood on a cock.
Just my own blood.
My parents died with hairstyles.
Periods messed them up.

REHAB HAIKU

Beer in a detention room.
Bug spray
To ruin a righteous bug.

DIVORCE

Updated information on injured persons spills my drink at
    every angle.
The reality of life is being married several times and
Having numerous affairs.

There was this collar my ex would put on me.
He would chain me to a table in the basement
And showcase me.

I probably could have undone it but I was
Fighting for reasons to emphasize
A somber nature scene.

JESUS IS A GALAXY FULL OF EARTHS

More female than woman. I've seen the YouTube video,
Less high than dog shit rolled in grass clippings.
I stay away from doctors and children and
It saves my sanity, life and money.
I'm miles from home, where shoes are scarce and teeth are even
   scarcer.
It takes the place of a penis in my dreams.
But coming back is necessary. And who's that coming up to
meet me?

It's me being dead.
And there's Rachel calling herself an absolute pubic hair.
She lists me
Drinking all night, buying whiskey after beer from her wand-
   hand.
I lick her pussy, lick her pussy, lick her pussy, end her pussy.
Rachel smokes
Arms with various moles.

Angels arc.
Music is bulging. Bulges trust licking.
I've fucked everyone gone mad,
Taken their diet tips from a gunshot wound to
No company has room for mistakes.
And a fat slut explains to a friend how to fuck another friend.
I'm real cool the rest of the night.

Fat sluts demand I fuckface.
When they want a system I'm right there with them.
I'm their lost lover
Beaching as a series of left hands that never shook.
I'm aware of their reason.
They're just another season.
I look beyond my disinterested lymph nodes.

I see my brother find love.
I see my sister pass to her children a day beyond compare.
I buy Rachel's dog shit life so I'm not forgot,
And we shake together and compete in all things.
I paste the penis of my dreams to
Video clips of her missing blinks.

ENNIS VOCATION

Omnipresent cattle raps
Seed all over my bed
An exhibitionist wheelchair babe.
I like cocaine.

And everybody likes our little baby
Cause when that child grows up
It's either a joystick or constantly boiling,
Both of which are in high demand.

Caucasian dogs accelerating their dog confines
Delude my daylight audition.
I'm homesick for nothing's named.

I bow in deep reverence to
A tasered YouTube confederation fingering me in the balls.
Yesterday was the same, and I think on my pillow on cocaine
That I'll cross off my schedule.
Life is too long to seek.

Life teaches suburban mechanical transparency.
It's that satisfying violence with a nutritious silence
Waiting in me.

A couple in an armchair is penetrated.
And now I sorta see too many parents.
Suburban mechanical transparency is the game naming
A lurking price-fixed blank thing.

Men set out within their submission.
Women develop a bottle to ease that submission.
A table plus a bottle plus a house plus light.
These are the rules thrown.

VACANT CLARITY

In the study where I pant, my meat accessorizes necks of teeth.
On my face are
Tribe-hunting tribes flashing simple thatched roofs
Sheltering leaves to bag and pubic hairs to shave.

Out of their loitering
Lash flashes of me losing my mind in a motel in the ground.

Golden mud enjoys my fall then beeps to dirty bits.
Adorns me with blacks and tans the cops shot.

And their dark bliss lays my cock in my skeleton.
My skeleton reveals the light of my eyes is logical toast.

We're on a washing machine, so lovingly
Dipping to cause a stain that lays a flappy collective
    consciousness cheese
Returning to its informal public user-defined tape.
Don't believe in anything you can't rape.

CIVILIZATION

A drag-hot hearse sunrise
Flea deploys its silent bliss.
Five violet leopards pray to that.

I'm five violent days jailed in an upright melon.
I make a face but hair loves nothing.
I make a face but get in line anyway.

A woman has her hair pulled into a steam cleaner.
A man has his scalp rushed to a blender.
I loathe life but live anyway.

My imagination plays coffin-shaker
And composes fast
Sophie and Kat tickling each other.

Kat pinches Sophie's flap.
A spider infuses eyeless pavement.
I have pussy envy.

Not being nowadays casts
My perfect union of felon and dull.
Burps from the lips of foreskin waterfalls,

Cola waterfalls, kerosene waterfalls,
Wire waterfalls, average waterfalls
Loathe life but get in line anyway.

Sophie and Kat know from long ago
A silent violet bliss.
I have eyeless envy.

APPENDIX

NO LIVES MATTER

7/11/16

~~SINGER/~~ SONGWRITER

SKELETON FOUND IN SUBURBAN HOUSE

A stray cat ~~attacked~~ attacks two people.
A garbage collector ~~tested~~ positive for rabies.
He's ~~could be~~ now part of a wild colony.

The skeleton of a man found at his daughter's
home
May have been there for eight years.
Police have been in my bedroom for three years.
My father's skeleton has ~~been~~ hospitalized
       at a psychiatric facility.

The stray cat will be dead in March.
It hasn't the vaguest notion what it's
       all for.
The skeleton of a man found at his daughter's
home is laughing mostly.

The fencelike vegetation transforms into
       an arena for a bloody struggle.
Clustered masses of mistakes... they have nostalgia
Pink ~~blooms~~ stab at the beast, for the infants.
Like a ~~cat~~ child's brain in a freezer.

A child's brain in a freezer
Saves me evenings and weekends.

FUCK STUCK

1/28/16 THE FAILURE OF REALITY

(1) IT OCCURS TO ME THAT SUICIDE OCCURS
        SHORTLY AFTER MY YOGA CLASS

SUICIDE OCCURS TO ME AFTER
                    MY YOGA CLASS

The old man at the table, how easily he remembers.
I'm just a girl from the city
Any intensely intelligent female artist I
            encounter
~~I simultaneously~~ admire and want to fuck.

(2) Do you wanna fuck?   FUCK STUCK
Function is the key.   stethoscope
The ~~voice~~ gotta drain.
Your intelligence has gotta stain. ~~stethe ste~~

        It urgently needs a new sense of
~~when Ichya fan is saying~~ all   stetho
People all color and ~~stet~~ size,—   car
Affected by a strange one more glass.
A spectacle of pain and silly souls.

(3) Gross nice and good entertainment.
~~A~~ Magic fingers drag a man from what's last
    I tried to see a life continuing to trade.
Then officers ~~stack all~~ faggots.
            stacked

emoji lied

10/22/16

BOMBS HIT KIDS MOURNING KIDS KILLED BY EARLIER BOMBS.

A street on feet arrives heroically.
The troll in the bathtub is its nose,
Have you ever forgotten how to piss while
contemplating lesbian sex?
You have blowfish arms.

~~[scribbled out line]~~

DIVORCE

Clumsy doll voice box
Feeds glaciers.
Hiding in the mountains
Where the bombs drop
The wanderers by raft,
They encounter
A worm with time to
Throw beach in its sleep,
Replaces guilt with passion and indifferen[ce]

+ hundred million beers infused with probe blood
spear scarecrows canning my vegetable burp.

ON THE WAY TO VISIT KAFKA'S GRAVE

I watched a Hare Krishna parade.
Met a French girl.
After lunch, she jerked me off.
Two hours ~~too~~ later we fucked on the bathroom floor
Second round lasted as long as the
         second coming of the messiah
    Thanks to my corporate edge.

A huge swarm of creatures at risk of starvation
Built the bridge I use to cross here to the
       circle-jerks   Ohio River.
Hare Krishna ~~jerk-offs~~ inflate my insides.
I'm talking total submission to the ways of
          flies thick on the floor
A series of me and my dishonest life.

    ~~The~~ Kafka's.
            my
On ~~my~~ way to visit Kafka's grave
There's very little food left in the world,
It must have seen something I ate.
On an island after the sun backs out
Balloon animals prefer infinite dirt.
~~Soul See interpret beautiful dreams.~~
I ~~expect~~ the same, forgiveness.

~~Skip~~ He's a child star who became an
      ugly adult at risk of starvation
Botched porch lights built the bridge I use
    To cross home to the Ohio River.

Like a Yeti waiting for me with his rod.
He's perfect in the post-season.

2/9/16   ~~SENIOR~~ MOMENT ~~T~~

I read about a man living on his mother's
        decomposing corpse in the bathtub.
In his front yard are shopping carts you can
    climb into to eat his mother out.

In her bathtub my Schopenhaur mask is
    our must-have born-again virgin.
He's perfect in the post-season.

Time will tell when I'm able to leave him
                    behind.
- Liked a Yeti decapitated by stained-glass
~~I SHOULD'VE BEEN IN BERLIN IN 1910~~
~~GIVE ME BACK MY TIME~~
    I WAIT FOR WHAT I DON'T KNOW
Yesterday on TV, a blowhole got away.
It dissolved into a keyhole that blew away.
And I was thrown into its can to do harm.
I began to never stay awake.
    I pulvarized blob
~~I've got~~ a ~~set~~ of sweatpants maxing out
        their credit cards ~~to blame~~. ~~starve~~
We're bound by the same ~~got it wrong~~.
Transfixed by otherworldly ATM dreams.
    never comprehend, ——— we will
The sunlight that filters through the leaves of
        trees ~~is~~ spiritual boredom.
        becomes

I wait up in the snark for you to
speak to me.
JACK BOWL BLOOD
GET COUPONS HERE

A NUMBER ON THE PHONE   4/18/

~~Can that work love to clean up~~

A face above the eye's world
Exposes businesses to other businesses.
An ear said its father just said
I want to begin the contest

If you ever want to find out about
somebody then hunt and fish with them.

Somebody hunts and fishes with him.

The dog finds debris in the woods.   coupon
He crawls out of a window to a locked
crawlspace is caught the next day.

I find my car been taken by a person I
found Money   know.

I find money is the person I know best.
It witnesses kills chickens
A rooster and ducks on my property.
You

My ~~time~~ is handling the baseball caps
soul   arrangements.

A MANNER OF RUNNING AROUND LIKE
A CHICKEN WITH ITS HEAD CUT OFF
your feeling LANGUAGE

babies, take me to the feeling
POEM ABOUT THE COLLAPSE OF LANGUAGE

1/22/16 DREAD

- Before eating, I pause to express appreciation
      for everything that is related to eating
- I am thankful that what I'm eating
      is tired.
- The sunlight that filters through the leaves
      of trees is spiritual boredom
- The cold wind that lets me know of winter's
      arrival ____
- The gentle sadness of my cigarette's
      passing
- Goes deep into the woods where everything
      is silent and peaceful
- What I'm eating is too mysterious and deep
      for words
- Awareness of the universe that triggers
      emotional responses that are too mysterious
   and deep for words.
- Accept that its out of control and move on
      with no regret.
- The ___ is more beautiful for having been
      broken
- A lust for a sizzling soap siren
Her face is packed with makeup.
Que more mellow, acoustic soul type of music.
The bruised basic power structure.

3/17/16

COFFIN'S have my
dick in their mouths

I'M EXPECTED TO HAVE A DICK IN MY MOUTH

- TABLES AMASS OF MY LIFE
     COFFIN'S have my dick in their mouths.
Tables do doubtful form.
Without a mind balancing beautiful tits.
Tables wear the maker of feeling my
                                      hand.

WORKING 7 TO 5 in
                True stables of doubtful barns.

STABLE

4/1/16

STABLE   I smile and say
                    the same picture
                          in my brain.

Coffins have my dick in their mouths.   I smile and
True stables in doubtful barns.   picture my
Dawn's already old at dawn.   brain in a
                                                     store
Coffin's inject their dicks in my mouth

For the bottles I drank last night,
Tables balance the feeling of my hand.
It's family owned, not franchised.
Dawn's break is at the store.
     Dawn breaks at the store. for more.

1/26/15

I WENT TO MEXICO I WENT
TO' CAMBODIA
To find relief from my the air / TO scale back my
Wolves in exploded places   homegrown pornogra
Build a nest fit for the vulture.
Holiness on the wolves in exploded places
        Fruit ripens on dogs.   Ripen on dogs
    - Disappearing into a predictable plot.
A wall of an airplane on fire
        Is my father.
    Elephants all taste of takeout burns
    Horrific umbrella of four snakes
Each face of wine dressed as a
                petrified forest.

A wall of an airplane on fire
    Builds a nest fit for the vulture.
                        a dead cartoon dude.
I sniff   a basket of ovaries.
I have 3 dicks and
This unemployment office is well-painted.
            an ma I burp up
Chesthair bacon.   Burped up.
Foot odor lives spine free.
    Sunken barn.   Mannequin cunt
    Mannequin asses — Endless
    Clouds of marrow, white endless cunts,
    I'll share the nothing I have to offer,
    then complain about what it said.
    I'm glad I'm a puppet.
    Space made of ants.
    Juices from the end of life.
        To saw apart my brain.

ACTIVE SHOOTER

~~I FEEL SICKENED BY THE HORROR THAT HAPPENED~~

I feel great all day.
I work.
I ~~conducted~~ ~~runs~~ out of beer.
I've only got so much time.

COUNTRY LIVING

Orgasms that live in the bones of the.
                    headless.

Earth of great fire.
My pedestrain conception which
          underlies my search for reality.

A virgin on the canvas imagined
          sucking cock.

4/23/14 2:32 AM
MODERN BUDDHISM

<s>PEE DRINK EAT</s>

Girl comes to live with her aunt & uncle who
she discovers is her uncle is her husband.
Scene deteriorates with 2 friends
as she meets her BF. into

Explosion after
Swim lessons after parents death
Eggs or thrown in the water at
the killer.

Kind of Bad Boy looking Killer.
Her Brother?
Shaking Woody or Fault guy?

Slide to the side like Names dashed
It may help to know that the Dali Lan
B a gun brand or something.

Some of these poems previously appeared in Fanzine, Gobbet, Paragraphiti, SCUD and Tragickal.

RC Miller lives in Metuchen, NJ and is the author of *Mask with Sausage*, *Pussy Guerilla Face Banana Fuck Nut*, the art book *Demon Drawings (all with Schism)*, and *Abstract Slavery* (Dostoyevsky Wannabe) co-written with Gary J. Shipley.

SC⛓ISM